**DO NOT REMOVE
CARDS FROM POCKET**

One, Two, Three, and Four. No More?

Catherine Gray   *Illustrated by Marissa Moss*

Houghton Mifflin Company   **Boston 1988**

To My Four:
Jim, Tammy, Michelle
and especially Jenny
C.G.

For Harvey—M.M.

Library of Congress Cataloging-in-Publication Data

Gray, Catherine.
    One, two, three, and four—no more?
Catherine Gray; illustrated by Marissa Moss.
    p.   cm.
    Summary: Twenty-two simple, rhyming verses depict animals who are
acting out a series of arithmetical relationships.
    ISBN 0-395-48293-3
    1. Counting—Juvenile literature. 2. Arithmetic—1961—Juvenile
literature. [1. Counting. 2. Arithmetic. 3. Animals.] I. Moss,
Marissa, ill. II. Title.
QA113.G7   1988   88-6827
513′.2—dc19   CIP
[E]   AC

Text copyright © 1988 by Catherine Gray
Illustrations copyright © 1988 by Marissa Moss

Printed in the United States of America

Y   10 9 8 7 6 5 4 3 2 1

One

One little cat
Can't find his hat.
It's not under the bed.
It's on his head.

Two

Two rollicking bears
On Grandma's favorite chairs.
Two chairs go *kerplunk*!
Two bears hiding in a trunk!

4

Three

Three baby bumblebees
Tumbled by a great big sneeze.
Next time, make sure it's a rose,
Not a clown's red, red nose.

5

Four

Four musical pigs
With four crazy wigs,
Playing their electric guitars.
Four rock 'n' roll pig stars!

One Pair

Two baby chimpanzees
Swinging from two coconut trees.
Trading places on a dare,
Two lumps make one pair.

Two Pairs

Four funny feet
Jogging down the street,
Resting on the stairs.
Four feet make two pairs.

One Plus One

One happy clam
Dines on pie and ham.
Up pops sister Sue.
1 + 1
Makes two.

One Plus Two

One proper lady ape
Tangled in a roll of tape.
Two monkeys try to set her free.
$1 + 2$
Is three.

One Plus Three

One little basset hound
Searching for his brother in the lost and found.
Who made that terrible snore?
$1 + 3$,
That's four!

Two Plus One

Hen and chick in their nest
Taking a quiet morning rest.
"Cluck, cluck!" says hen. "Oh, glory be!"
$2 + 1$
Makes three.

Two Plus Two

Two fuzzy mittens,
Two crying kittens.
Mama knits two mittens more.
$2 + 2$,
That's four!

Three Plus One

Three skating mice
Making figure eights on ice.
One fat rat slides through the door.
Crash!
$3 + 1$
Makes four.

Four Minus One

Four jumping frogs
Bouncing on four logs.
One leaped up to a tree.
$4 - 1$
Leaves three.

Four Minus Two

Frederick J. Fox
Wore four tiger-striped socks.
Two disappeared without a clue.
$4 - 2$
Leaves two.

Four Minus Three

Four mischievous flies
Eating big bear's pies.
Three said, "That honey's more fun!"
Splat!
$4 - 3$
Leaves one.

17

Three Minus One

Three hippos frolicking on the beach,
Building sand castles as high as they can reach.
One hippo sneezed, "Ah . . . Achoo!"
3 – 1
Leaves two.

Three Minus Two

Three ballerina cows
Taking their final bows.
Two dance off in the setting sun.
$3 - 2$
Is one.

Two Minus One

Crazy Lucy Goose
Had two teeth that were loose.
She tied one to a tree and broke into a run.
$2 - 1$
Leaves one.

Four

Four elephants having fun
Beneath the hot tropical sun.
But late that night they did find
Four elephants a bit red behind!

Three

Three skunks busily doing their chores,
Bottling perfume for perfume stores.
Three bottles tipped on their noses.
"Eeyuck! We smell like three sweet red roses."

Two

Two cute prancing deer
Practicing a football cheer.
Two deer leap and spin around.
Two tangled deer upon the ground.

One

One small bear down by the brook
Curled up with his favorite book.
Reading about one, two, three, and four.
No more.